THE ISLAND

THE ISLAND

Haiku for my 33rd Birthday

Oscar d'Artois

shabby doll house

First published by Shabby Doll House

June 2024
www.shabbydollhouse.com
@shabbydollhouse

THE ISLAND

Cover & interior illustrations by Mad Manning
Cover & interior design by Lucy K Shaw
Translated by Christopher Seder

Set in Garamond

ISBN: 978-1-7379242-6-5

ILLUSTRATED BY

MAD MANNING

for Jordan DeBor

CONTENTS

"Hey, hey," he sang softly, "hey, to eat black bread with farmhands, to ride horses bareback over a meadow..."

- Witold Gombrowicz, *Ferdydurke*

The Bridge Over the Rio Salado

The province of Cádiz lies on the somewhat lesser-known Atlantic coast of the autonomous community of Andalusia. Between Cádiz city and the town of Conil de la Frontera, there are a series of marshlands and salt beds lined with old aqueducts, pink flamingos, and small rock huts in ruin, with many of their roofs caved in.

The town of Conil stands on a hill overlooking a beach, the *Playa de Los Bateles*. This beach's considerable size makes it a popular spot for sunset walks among locals and tourists alike. It stretches out west for a few miles, then ends abruptly when it runs into a series of red cliffs. If you continue up onto these cliffs, you will find yourself immersed in a sprawling, bumpy plateau of red clay, a veritable Martian landscape. The cliffs are thought to be the historical home of the monster Geryon, who was said to have dwelt in the far West of the Mediterranean, near the garden of the Hesperides. This was the end of the known world for the Greeks and Romans: there was *Mare Nostrum* – 'our sea' – and then the mysterious, terrifying Beyond that was the Atlantic.

Indeed, the ancient name for Cádiz is 'Gades,' which, if you follow the logic of the linguistic tic common in certain Spanish dialects of allowing the voiced velar plosive /g/ to lazily slide from the glottis down into the back of the throat and into the voiceless pharyngeal fricative /h/, you might infer corresponds to Hades – or, at least, to its gates.

This sense of being at the end of the known world is further compounded by the fact that many towns in the region have, like Conil, the suffix *'de la Frontera'* appended onto the end of their name – meaning 'of the border,' or frontier. This more specifically refers to their being at the end of Christendom, since during the latter part of the

Reconquista these were the much-raided border towns between the Crown of Castile and what remained of the Caliphate of Granada, the last Moorish stronghold on the Iberian Peninsula.

Yet it is hard not to think of it as also referring to the *frontera* with the ocean, separating the whole of Eurasia from the lands that lie beyond, the far-off island archipelagoes that emerge in the lead-up to the Americas.

The Strait of Gibraltar is located a little further eastward down the coast. Hercules is said to have created the strait by using his superhuman strength to smash a path through the Atlas Mountains, rather than cross them, opening up the waterway between the Atlantic and the Mediterranean in the process. He did this while on his way out west to go find Geryon, as he had been commanded to do for his 10th labor, to slay the monster and make away with the red cattle he kept on his equally red lands. Whether Hercules actually did this out of revenge following a lovers' spat, and why he thought it would be easier to smash and then presumably swim across a mountain range, rather than simply hike it, are both topics that remain the subject of some debate among scholars.

East of the town lies another beach, the *Playa del Castilnovo,* which stretches out long and flat as far as the eye can see. The only visible landmark aside from the hills further inland and, on a clear day, the Atlas Mountains of Morocco silhouetted in the distance, is a single abandoned watchtower. The tower has black holes where its windows once were. The roof is gone. Crows circle it constantly, and a shy, endangered species of ibis has made it a preferred nesting ground, perhaps due in part to the fact that it is located miles away from any human habitation.

A nearby plaque explains that the tower is all that remains of an old Moorish fort, much of which was destroyed during the tsunami that followed the Lisbon earthquake of 1755. It was subsequently used as a *miradór* by local fishermen to look out for tuna fish as they made their way down the Atlantic coast and through the strait of Gibraltar to their breeding grounds in the Mediterranean. Tourism aside, this tuna was and remains the town's primary bread and butter – many local specialties are based on it, and they ship it as far away as Japan.

The town is split off from the *Playa del Castilnovo* by a small river, known as the *Rio Salado*, or salty river. Before the bridge over the river and the nearby road were built, the story goes, the land beyond it was almost entirely cut off from civilization, accessible only by wading through the river when it wasn't flooding. This allowed the village of El Palmar to flourish, out of sight and out of mind, a few miles further down the beach past the abandoned tower.

Built-up largely by hippies in the '70s who were seeking to live an off-the-grid life outside of the then-Francoist society (the memory of which persists in the form of disused bunkers that pepper the entire coastline), the village is a collection of huts that were cobbled together using a combination of corrugated metal, red bricks, and even the occasional thatched roof.

While nowadays a relatively trendy surfer's getaway, and a party spot in the summer months, the village continues to have an unusually wild feel to it for Western Europe – if for no other reason than that its existence is something of a sore spot for the municipality of the more conservative nearby hill town it depends on, which refuses to supply El Palmar with reliable electricity and drinking water. Its inaccessibility and lack of policing also make it a hotspot for certain illicit activities, a fact that may contribute both to the resentment and to the wildness.

Of course, there are other ways to access El Palmar – by boat, for instance – and the river never seems to get that deep: at low tide, you can usually just walk across it without getting your boardshorts wet. Nevertheless, this is how the story of El Palmar's existence-outside-existence gets told.

And the sense of there being something untamed about it extends to the stretch of sand that lies between it and the Rio Salado, too. As a result, that beach remains largely untouched compared to the town beach that people flock to on their walks.

You won't find a single *chiringuito*, the beach bars that line the other beachfront, on it, for instance. But you're far more likely to encounter flotsam and jetsam: stray pieces of wood, large plastic jugs, and sometimes even deflated dinghies. When you happen upon the latter it is impossible not to wonder: To whom did it belong? Was it carrying migrants, drugs, or something else entirely? Whoever they were, does the washed-up boat's presence mean they made it, or that they didn't? It seems an awfully long way up the coast to be coming from Africa in an inflatable raft, but then maybe that means the coastline here is slightly less guarded? Under cover of night, with the old watchtower acting as a landmark, it does seem like an ideal place to come ashore and make a break for it, far from any barriers or town centers. But so, as much of a surfer's paradise as El Palmar may be, the dinghies serve as a reminder that the ocean is more than just a place where people play in the waves.

The beach is, finally, of the two, the 'clothing optional' one. If you're going to El Palmar, on a day when the beach is not being battered by the Levante – the 'tourist-clearing' wind, which lifts up long tendrils of sand and snakes them down towards the water, – you are likely to spot a few people taking this option to heart, slumped like beached whales under parasols up near the dunes. That is, if they are not actual beached creatures, like the eight-foot tuna that sometimes wash up on the shore and stay there to rot until the gulls take an interest or the sea swallows them up again.

But most people don't go this way. When they head down to the beach at dusk, they go westward, in the direction of other people, of cafés, and of the clear cut-off point the cliffs at the end provide.

Still, the eye is invariably drawn towards the bridge, with the occasional silhouette of a lone figure standing on it, and beyond it the cattle farm, the moon rising above the red bull mural on the old white barn, and in the distance the hills, the tower, the ocean, the islands.

THE ISLAND

Ukrainian flag

in the grindr bio : nice !

autoerotic

lack of punctuality

– « time bender » ; that's me ! –

casting off webs in my wake

a constellation

of cocks drawn across the sky

shooting stars : cum streaks

against the black firmament

i'm a nebula

anarchia nervosa

so thin it implodes

adorn my body with it

balefire river

it is my 33rd spring

my god… it's ok ??

i usually hate it

but this spring's giving

threatening & slutty – hot

the word man inspires

only ire/pity in me

but i'm sick to death

of poems where they just invent

new quirky genders

the man from across the street

has a dog who barks

like it wants to rip my guts

out into its mouth

& part of me's like yes bitch

go for it, please just

relieve me of this meatsack

core me insides out

trim me down to ivory

my new theory on

tipping : it's BDSM

it's like when i was

a sailor ; people would pay

for the privilege

to ride with us a few days

« learn the ropes » of how

to wash the galleys & heads

scrubbing on their knees

worshiping our working ways

what i mean is we

all need a farmboy to be

slavish towards you see

i love my own abjection

A lot of my friends

are saying they just want to

write things for their friends

which i can relate to yes

i want to speak to

my friends in a secret voice

a language outside

language, straight from the void/womb

we all relate to

but what about trying to

bring the face of god

demonic tearing its way

back through the fabric

of reality, tear down

the scaffold, unveil

the ugly parts too, you know

i feel i haven't

felt a real feeling in years

I'm trying to get

at something so obvious

yet out of my reach

but my best thoughts i forget

immediately

flaming trash heap of my mind

time to face the facts :

organic nut butters suck.

sometimes, expensive

things are just worse & that's that

i guess what is key

is to always remember

there is an island

an island of hopes & dreams

where the clouds look like

pictures of clouds on bright days

where the coconuts

taste like how you'd want them to

where death is on pause

where strangers hold hands & smile

where they lounge & bathe

a fortress of frolicking

Burgundy is like :

old dudes drinking in their cars

tags like suck it bitch

ACAB & anarchy on

smashed office windows

i walk around like some kind

of ancient teen, broke

ass soles & broken thing i

wouldn't call a soul

digital no man baby

boylife in EU

well that's what happens when you

up & move away

after a few years the friend

nucleus loosens

but hey everyone's alone

in the whirl of their

own world girl do u feel me

Island shops are like :

under-buttered garlic bread

offensively priced

cobblestoned fantasies of

socialized healthcare

an island can be dreadful

for an outsider

heliophilic nightmare

if life ever gets

how it gets all u need is

sun & a river

to stand in & scream babe &

every day i

bathe in my river like i

think i'm the goddamn

little mermaid, seems unfair

to the river what

about it does it have a

river to bathe in ?

« Infinite wrath & despair » –

something i wanted

tattooed on my ass for years ?

well, i'm 33

& all my friends are getting

divorced or married

or pregnant – good luck i guess

cookies for breakfast

cuz i just don't give a fuck

emo tornado

the chestnut blossoms are out

& they are making

me sneeze obnoxiously loud

(it's a condition

my wife calls my attention

seeking disorder)

this is how i know it is

my fucking birthday

Jesus year conniption fit

April in Paris

arpeggios of feeling

Mostly i'm small but

sometimes i think i'm the sun

subsuming others

in my delirious real

so i'm 33

an addiction to stretching

a shock of grey hair

is all i can show for it

my mind's still insane

my body still craves the same

& my heart o well

that's bottomless maybe but

what's more romantic

than splitting a whole baguette

seeing old people

just ask for a half one

at the bakery

is sad u think but i think

it's touching, really

that it's a nationally

accepted request

In a way it is wondrous
this campy outpost
& in another way it's
erosion kept at
bay by billions of bucks &
the bodies of those
who erect faux-rustic shacks
down here on the ground
gay heaven is a business
but still an island
glittering distant promise
always receding
so i wander despondent
rush to yoga class
chug $12 iced coffees
i « perform labor »
i mean i do perform it
spend long nights switching
the thoughts of one person to

another's language

my job is to go abstract

be a non-presence

which is ideal for feeling

like a non-presence

so i say my prayers at night

to Janus patron

saint of two-faced openings

shimmering ghosts but

why'd i bother building this

eternal yoga

temple that's my body if

not for the island

all things beautiful must be

abandoned i think

as i sigh my way out of

the coffee shop door

My scale says « happy new year ! »

i drag my laptop

charger round like a blanky

o not me back on

my dark night of the soul shit

arrow stopped mid-flight

It’s not like there aren’t other

beaches in my life

mimosa-lined too just in

different ways where i

can solo rave in the dunes

But why do some texts

just matter more than others

& how could i not

wither before them, with their

greater existence…?

& experience all my worst

inklings re : my life

& the world's nature as truth ?

Hence why i must stretch

hence why i silent suffer

hence my abjection

So pour the wine & whiskey

coat me in coffee,

cigarettes, hell, cbd !

or fuck me up babe

with fundamentalism

wrapped in trendy furs

atop a unicorn throne

gimme catholic

schoolboy angst & guilt, fascist

impulses to kill

my body's soft animal

tell me that desire

is movement & movement is

suffering ; stillness

& withdrawal their antidote

the only one babe

there's no spirituality

where self-punishment

isn't featured babe so fuck

spirit out of me

if the alternative's just

say no to matter

we're here on earth to loiter

funny kinda curse

that when we left the water

we'd have to seek it

out to quench our endless thirst

gum & perfume spray

to cover the cigarette

smoke stench for u babe

like some 13-year-old girl

my yoga teacher

tells me i must do tapas

he is spanish but

no he doesn't mean eating

he means more the fire

of self-denial used to

make you indifferent

to if you have this or that

he says this will lead

me to be able to see

god in all beings

& things – so here's a fun game

i play when i'm bored :

i try to see each being

as a little god

& then wonder to myself

what's that god up to ?

this achieves very little

but is fun i guess

kaleidoscope of halos

i do a trick where

i pretend a public bike

is broken so i

can reuse it when i need

i'm thinking about

how much i hate the metro

in Paris & then

about how good we have it

in Paris versus

say New York public transport

& then wondering if

art thrives in socialism ;

who can be blasé

with all these new fun flavors

of chips to try out ?

i mean of course like i hate

capitalism

i guess but if i think the

living conditions

that it creates for artists

foster suffering

& that this in turn fosters

creativity

then do i hate it really ?

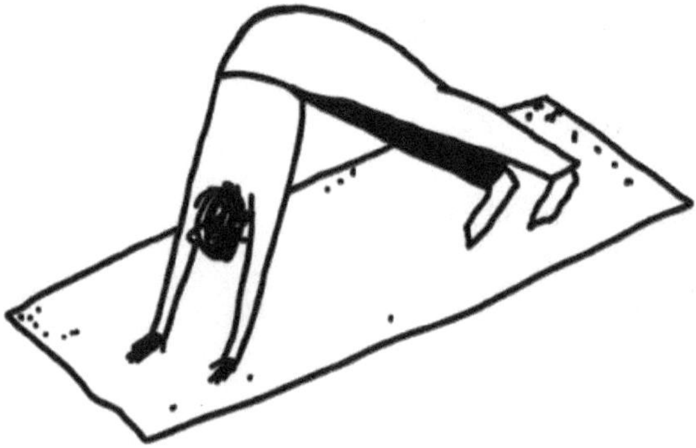

The pizza hot sauce

is called « hot pizz » – i'm turned on ?

my phone says to do

my steps so i do & feel

like a sim in sim

city bitch (sim sim city

bitch) watching people

walk dogs down their glittering

high rise garden paths

spandex legs & massive smiles

of course yes i dream

of deification in

avatar form but

posing on social media

is libidinal

being off it as a pose

is libidinal

too probably we should all

leave society

tho i've yet to meet two groups

with the same idea

of why & just what that means

Like I'm terrified

as well at the idea of

sincere expression

if i seize empire's words

guzzle them right down

my throat regurgitate them

will they lend me their

power will i become empire ?

ensoul me with plague

spit it out into my mouth

I've just got bad vibes

on the bus i want silence

sorry about my

aggressive nihilism

it just consumes me

no not me dreaming stupid

dreams of producing

the void of wanting to be

bathed to be washed out

in wave after pink wave of

electronic screams

Still how simple life would be
if others would just
not exist stop disturbing
the limpid surface
of this transient existence
we were flung into

There's a spider in my back

there is abjection

its deliciousness & then

there's wanting a kiss

arpeggios of cleaving

i hate the spring cuz

it reminds me of falling

new thirst demons bloom

i bike past a slaughterhouse

discomfort swelling

America just feels like

a waste of money

I get lonely & call up

a friend who reminds

me how we had to sharpie

every sin we could

think of on our bodies once

& what do i make

of that ? she asks but the truth's

i don't make much as

i don't recall it at all

A rainy tuesday

races brutally my way

wasn't prepared for

how it'd pin me to the bed

smacked into blankness

staring at dried red flowers

against a white wall

arpeggios of silence

if i think of my

self dreaming of the island

my abnegation

i am almost moved to tears

but can't quite get there

see myself looking distant

in the train window

symphonic devastation

seagull flight in grey

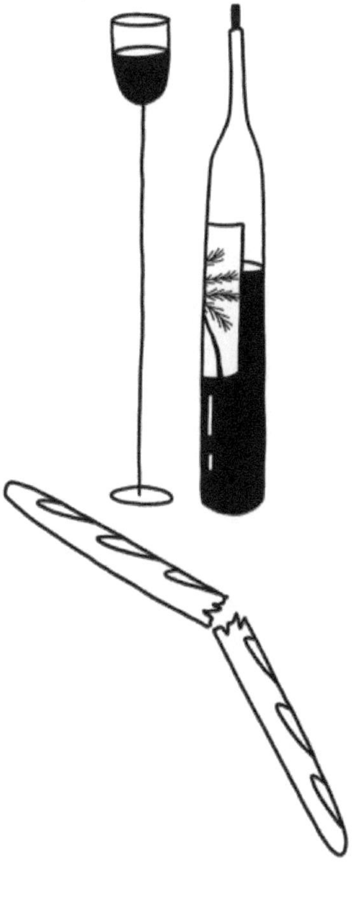

Party supplies to wreck me :

my fucking birthday

a grave that reads « SANSOUCIS »

occupy the vibes

Vanessa Carlton moshpit

pumpkin spice grey sweats

day moon over bull mural

indulgent trailmix

extremely advanced sunset

opiate moonscape

sentimental mug owning

altar for jock socks

unabashed cross-legging

ghosts of sunflowers

melancholy sky penis

vaping laserbeams

my seltzer graveyard belly

chilled red, pure seaglass

sunwind on soft skin now you're

talking my language !

archipelago of pain

we call experience

lit candle torrential rain

greek temple at dawn

tree lined path star-studded sky

when i go back to

cities i can't remember

how to be-with or

how people even speak so

lying in the dark

in a room full of strangers

i take sick pleasure

in opening my eyes ohm

peace motherfuckers

what i mean's any thing is

a thing that contains

its own opposite you know

blossoms are dying

chastity is horniness

a company called

Translate By Humans' secret

is they use machine-

translation liberally

black holes are lurking

in the hearts of giant stars

i'm cute when nasty

yoga can make me anxious

tell me to relax

i will when it's time to stop

palm tree heavens leave

me whipped raw by compulsion

& then when they don't

i think myself a martyr

bleeding, ascending

my own pink cloud rhapsody

an opera house

at the bottom of a lake

imploding lotus

blablablablablablabla

No nightmares baby

sunbleached arm hairs boardwalk breeze

hypomanic joy

butterfly corpse on the screen

so we go to sea

naked swimming like a prayer

i'll take you there o

jk like Jonas with tan

lines & an anklet

i'll raise the sky to the ground

drain the sea just for

a single drop of island

Poseidon-in-pearls

will i ever get back there

& suppose i did

could i also find my way

back on the low-lit

path to the home of our minds

What i mean is still

there are perfect days of surf

sun beer snacks sex so

render me into the storm

full moon hurricane

what did the thunder whisper

right into my gut

Backbend me into nothing

maybe it was when

we threw the paper blue box

that had been grandma

into the island's waters

watched it float briefly

before dissolving that it

caught me in its grip

the trouble with my face is

it accumulates

yearnings like past ghosts floating

by in subway cars

a donkey at the Loire beach

mingles with river

folk a beluga swims up

the seine to Paree

the rivers are drying up

& god we're thirsty

the orcas come for our boats

our rudderless lives

sure let the yachts burn, we say

with nowhere to go

but surfboards maybe if it's

warm enough to swim

I mean there's more to life than

drinking out of jars

but hey congratulations

for bringing along

your personal metal straw

All of my friends come

up to visit finally

we put on a play

but i am too distracted

& spend the whole time

yearning for an island where

boys run obsessed with

this quiet devastation

of my invention

moisturizing mournfully

i dream of a rave

at the end of the rainbow

moon beach peach orgy

lush as fuck but if i went

i'd spoil the dream right ?

that's the thing with the island

it recedes again

forever moving away

the island of course

is not real, a construct of

imagination

it's not like i've never been

but there's a difference

between how i represent

it in my mind's eye

& how things actually are

do i have to spell

it out for u baby like

crass jokes at drag shows

not an apotheosis

in aquamarine

so maybe best it recedes

& i'll learn to love

the reversed prism of it

in rearview mirrors

So we go to the beach but

swimming is banned &

if that's not the frenchest thing

i watch two boys horse

around in the sand the blond

joke humping his friend

clearly in love parasols

flap birds screech at them

there is an architecture

I find the perfect

denim jacket but it has

no pockets – that's life

(i still buy it anyway)

the heatwave never

materializes the cool

mist machines just dance

alone in grey air – that's life

i apply for what

i think will be salvation

(read : a yoga camp)

a different island i guess

i'm rejected – that's

the crumbling of mountains

melting ice cream cone

of my tiny little mind

what new life to lead

what new idol can i throw

myself at now to

receive the voice of prophets

i just need one kick

to go on reaffirming

that the space beyond

hands is also part of hands

Set my life on fire

with sporty street poet-wear

immediately

PETRICHOR knuckle tats o

well, it almost works

it's true that poetry's a

vow of poverty

that's why it's so middle class

sing to me o muse

slam me into the counters

seppuku baby

Victorian drama queen... ?

it's my damn birthday

the hell does it matter if

i speak in some voice

i've got closets in closets

all the way down babe

all smoke & masks that masc masks

all scene adjacent

all poet influencer

all class enemy

I'd become sure the magic

8-ball was speaking

the truth to me in secret

staked my life on it

it had told me i'd get in

but lied to me ?! now

another island denied

i'm all *shock !* *horror !*

so i go to my sports app

sign up for a class

just called « self-realization »

(45 minutes)

& eat noodles with my hands

straight out of the fridge

then start looking into new

life escape valves stat

half dora the explorer

half vampire slut

no i don't want to be like

this but purity

is so goddamn tedious

& not an option

So i'm feeling murderous

as hell all crop-topped

out in the supermarket's

fancy hummus aisle

that's cities for you baby

don't ever show me

a man – i'll simply throw up

when did i become

this fountain of bitterness

christ rid me of this

PhD in grudge-holding

sometimes all i'd need

is a screw straight in one ear

& out the other

to radiate tendrils of

kindness, scarves of love

Aphrodite-in-shell style

Forget a poem

i want waterfalls of rocks

to be possessed by

skewer me like Sebastian

who doesn't love ruins

of interiority

pull me apart make

floating shards of this body

my stretching mantra

wrist brace but make it fashion

to show i suffer

o i'm so very fragile

who will hold my hand

Midwinter aperol spritz

simply existing

here feels like a money pit

the problem is with

the landscapes in New England

there's no room for awe

just godless people desperate

to feel guilt for stuff

in the shower i stare at

one daddy long legs

tryna eat a smaller one

i think, « yass, daddy »

tho i'm not sure at which one

Exhausting ! to be

always so devoured by

« my identity »

roughly free as a werewolf

howled into being

i'll tell u the difference

between love & lust :

one is something crushing &

inescapable

the other's... well, anyway

helps to remember

Satan's pride was also put

inside him by god

Nail me to the crystal sea

i can put on white

undies so i can feel clean

at least & then let

the waistband stick out a bit

so others know too

even tho no one will see

daydream of nights of

recklessness in concrete heat

tits out & mumbling

every time we touch i get

this feeling so pass

the chrysanthemum wine bathe

me in moonwater

to preserve this cracked skin since

one problem i have

is i can only really

conceive of others

as lovers or not at all

I chop this poem

into 10,000 pieces

shove them in a pouch

that doesn't close so they go

flying everywhere

as i fly cross the world cuz

i only engage

with the divine when trapped in

mid-air turbulence

think i can control the plane

if i just promise

to devote my ablutions

to It once i land

half of my whole life is gone

fling me at a tower

enraged i pick you flowers

hope a boar gores me

o the island the island

i sigh at the wind

say the sounds 'til they're nothing

but widening gaps

the island i think's saudade

on steroids always

irretrievable like that

awkward moment when

you know you'll never not be

startled to be flung

into your life the way wheels

on a car can seem

to go backwards in slo-mo

as it drives past you

there is an architecture

Poets will tell you

crazy shit like « yes, the Spring

needed us to be »

rave about the mystery

of abandoned towers

i mean why not a sunset

so gorgeous it caused

societal collapse how

disappointing i'm

that metaphysical bitch

i'm always screaming

« i need a tower ! » – like what

i mean's a feast of

solitude unleashed in space

red maple rivers

I want to have a poem

that feels like iron

like steel like something u bite

down on & the blood

comes gushing out but it just

feels so fucking good

a book like a scream also

like coming out of

a dark wood & being like

o hell yeah i love

my love & i'm dancing &

i'm surfing & i

can live it it's all ok

a poem that's queer

but not so much in the sense

of being concerned

with identity as in

the original

sense of perverting the world

i want a poem

between me & whatever

ur-freak i call god

& my friends on some kinda

metaphysical

plane we all share a poem

like the infinite

fluorescent thrum beat that gets

your heart roaring when

you're on the road listening

to bangers & you're

way too full of it all just

sitting there insane

a poem that feels like an

autotuned angel

of death in a sunshower

but how'd you put that

on a page ? want it to steal

shamelessly, try on

voices gleefully revel

in it find itself

differently for it want for

it to rocketlaunch

people right into the stars

to bare the guts of

my oddity like a pink

flamingo head cocked

& for others maybe to

see themselves in that

i want it confessional

not as in sorry

but as in screw you & then

also like a door

where you could step in behind

this or that sea of

blank faces on the subway

their minds barreling

thru unknown cloudscapes yes have

i said it enough

times for my teeth to turn to

interstellar wires

For a year i couldn't stand
melon, a favorite
a taste change likely caused by
the virus i guess
that's just the price u pay for
seeing friends in flesh
digital no man baby
tho i guess it's wild
how we can talk across worlds
thru portals of sand
just make me dimensionless
hair like a gravestone
& a year 'til i can go
back to the island
so cancel my mind with all
consuming dinner
feasts smother me in cheeses
fry my neurons babe
the best part about giving
in to something is

it frees you of it briefly

A tsunami of

longing at exposed ankles

nothing to cry for

i lie on the floor while you

try the new vacuum

out & act like « oh, no, help –

aaaah ! it's pulling me

away !!! » – we do have a laugh

After the flood i

stopped caring anymore i

told myself this life

couldn't be so insanely

contained or i'd burst

so yes i let my head loll

on a denim thigh

i thought plz plz plz let me

get what i wanted

tho after so much absence

was it that even ?

public like a small garden

frog statue clutching

its stone heart i croaked take this

& prayed forgiveness

I say flood. i mean virus

two years in a box

early onset middle age

the all-sucking black

hole from which nothing remains

but a memory

of being nothing sweaty

cramped shoulders white cloud

amethyst palaces you

dwelt in whatever

let me the fuck out split me

open with the light

Even tho yes i confess
the vibes here can be
immaculate in this too
small home we were moved
to by the virus, when there
are summer showers
outside & we stream Chopin
share burrata bowls
in this bright colored cove at
the end of the world
but god babe please not one more
sight of this damn town

I need shimmering bodies

jumping off sailboats

& then to be alone 3

to 5 business months

transatlantic loneliness

amnesia baby

show me what it's like for you

the fucking forest

let another darkness speak

fantasy of being

barefoot leather jungle dirt

princess running thru

the island pines fucking god

how we spin around

it sucks us in – if we let

it take us, why not ?

Digital no man baby

i go for weeks at

a time without talking to

people so sometimes

what comes out is a squeal like

a panicked saw chained

to a violin's entrails

sorry about me

funny how we order things

in some ways shoulders

are like your top hips, you know

scientists have been

shooting jellyfish in space

& now they hate it

back on earth gravity's tug

a nightmare to them

tell me how can i get back

show me i dare you

bro an experience of life

that isn't mania

i mean the real life that is

the life that isn't

somewhere else even tho real

life is – or is it ?

which is where angels come in

möbius rivers

A new virus comes & bars

me from the island

so i order 300

pairs of cute short shorts

off amazon for revenge

i stay up late nights

unable to forget this

man with a crater

in his face & a t-shirt

that said « summer vibes »

sure a pimple's killing me

& feel pissed at god

i get so excited when

the recycling truck

picks everything up these days

girl do u feel me

And why's shipping so pricey

when people strive to

keep things local what they mean

is we'd love to stay

in the heart of empire, thanks !

sorry is that mean

what i mean is nobody

believes in queerness

not like a bedrock or fire

It’s so beautiful

upstate i might stop breathing

& simply combust

i pass a tiny island

in the middle of

the Hudson river, really

a rock with one small

amber tree on it i want

to memorialize

it forever, no reason

but that it happened

it doesn't matter but then

what does, so it does

i passed a tiny island

in the mid-Hudson

I throw myself at friday

when sunday comes I'm

tired of life's razor-sharp bite

have pie in the park

crave a gentle kind of bond

an ease with strangers

I also need blueberries

cozy vibes a soft

made up language for us to

speak amongst ourselves

7 years of cuddles just

to face the day so

Take on your problems with grace,

bitch ! i say shaking

myself like i want to shake

some other things like

i don't know a cop maybe

altho i don't want

to shake anyone really

I started yoga

to cure hangovers but now

it's a religion

or addiction which really

what's the difference

overwhelmed is my lifestyle

i stop two pigeons

nesting on the windowsill

by stealing their egg

i crack the egg in the sink

most un-yogicly

it looks like a normal egg

i think should i eat ??

& feel racked with guilt for days

Controlling my gut :

it sure beats contemplating

the eternal sea !

« let the ground sink in your sweat »

– my guru again –

i mean i wish i could drench

it subsume it like

honestly it’s exhausting

keeping up with these

rituals my mind is sure

are the point of life

but babe eternal twinkhood

doesn’t come free, right ?

for whom do i stretch, really ?

everyone senses

their personal care routine

is self-indulgence

mindless vain & selfish, right ?

No nightmares baby

Artaud thought the only way

to get rid of god's

immanent gaze was to shit

him out properly

which just sounds like an eating

disorder, really ?

like i accept my organs

or i want to try

to love them at least pretend

to dwell embodied

Poetry sailing travel :

my library aisle !

so i hurl myself manic

empyrean whirlwind

guinea pig from place to place

do you remember

Berlin, walking on the edge

of a sidewalk &

asking each other do you

think angels are bliss -

fully unaware of their

angelicity

just people walking around

mediocre, blessed

to be blind to their beauty

hard not to wonder

were we talking about us

watching the cameras

zooming out of our bodies

the violins strike

up their lascivious score

At the beach it's light

blinding on water by day

firefly forest

fairytale dusk ; i still find

ways to feel depressed

i make sourdough tho it's

not cool anymore

arpeggios of kneading

mold like a Pollock

hear the horny cicadas

twist & bend the sun

such tumultuous silence

i become obsessed

with the notion the island

will cure me altho

i know better than most that

we lug the baggage

of ourselves from place to place

that a place is not

a panacea but still

am i not allowed

one coconut of respite

maybe it's fiction

that it's a portal to being

what i do is i

get taken with an idea

to reinvent life

meanwhile life is just waiting

for me on the porch

or its accumulation

is anyway just

waiting for me to notice

its spiderweb threads

caught only in certain light

is that not enough

it urges tho the question

hangs there in midair

And then winter's like steamroom

cut vein fantasy

so i put sunglasses on

in the pouring rain

& think : take from me the skin

The spatula says

« BE THANKFUL » like a slap threat

it's a whole ass vibe

So overwhelmed with nothing

i remember heat,

a skatepark, shirts off, lounging

hands under waistbands

translucent t-shirts behind

the pizza oven

at work, trying to make it

across the country

on foot only to make it

from Bos- to Brock-ton

stealing gas station sandwich

sleeping under firs

only to be towed away

Two seagulls feasting

on a pigeon's carcass, « oh ! »

your child points, giggling

later he says, « i'll always

be with you, pigeon »

Death by year-end fave book lists

as a child i thought

heaven was a library

now i hate reading

i remember this one dream

a midnight blue room

bearded guy behind a desk

him asking me what

animal or plant i'd like

to live as this time

there is an architecture

death by watching you

pull an old lady's suitcase

up the subway stairs

gulped down by pairs of strange eyes

thru the evening rain

« you just love your own yearning »

death by biking past

offensively hot strangers

crashing down the stairs

flinging myself at trains so

when i race on past

the Louvre belting out pop songs

from the early aughts

yes it is a cry for help

I mean i could live

like a saint lug god around

thru deserts, rivers

but that takes being grounded

i'm as stable as

a ferret on nitrous gas

do i need others

so i can hear myself or

to drown myself out ?

i mean who cares what others

think I can just go

& howl « love me ! » at the moon

friend criticizes

another friend for being

narcissistic to

the point of clinically

being unaware

of the needs of others which

is funny because

that's exactly the problem

that you see in them

i say we love to critique

others for the parts

we dislike most in ourselves

& feel briefly like

i can see my own failings

Paris is like men

vaping by on e-scooters

cathartic croissant

i wear tie dye one day &

someone spits on me

summer starts in September

for me altho yes

the fall does slip its way in

that's just how it is

things are slipping in & out

of each other all

the time everywhere each thing

its own undoing

i want so bad to show you

what the world's made of

untangle the matrix of

the universe hung

over in a bucket hat

how when we speak it's

others speaking our convos

a dialogue of

thousands reverbing thru us

red maple cisterns

how there's an architecture

molten gold veins that

run through the body & trees

bridges archways of

half-remembered sound that hold

this house together

as much as the next ghost does

send me back into

those rivers babe let me drink

from a world-viewing

untarnished by merciless

begging for the next

thing and the next like ever

more glittering globs

of pearls bloody unending

thick as walls get back

to where i dove into out

on the rocks – but don’t

let me think one’s sacred at

the other’s expense

give me the strength to find joy

in gazing up at

a face of horrifying

beauty eternal

as i am not love loving

love you know teacher

milkfeed me the beyond like

how at the shitty

river beach ’80s concert

in a circus tent

button downs buttoned way down

warm nights / warm beer to

recognize the ascension

nymph-into-tree-style

in the old french line dancers

for what it is – have

the grace to be grateful for

happiness sinking

tear the backward mirrored sun-

glasses off my face

let me feel the thrill of your

small eternity

I don't know, watching you walk

into the water

your dress hiked up to your knees

backlit in the sun

life always just out of reach

My friend says going

to the island makes him feel

fucking psychotic

he got a panic attack

onboard the ferry

he says what it is is that

you put 10,000

drug-addled inverts desperate

for the sunset beach

fuck of their lives transcendent

finally enough

to say now i can die that

is begin to live

plus there's nowhere you can go

on a decent run

So what if nature offers

itself up smiling

in its totality still

my wife on the phone

to a friend who is struggling

makes me upset – why ?

maybe we're all manchildren

who just need babies

so we can shut up, grow up

like aren't i too old

to chase fantasies & whine

about loneliness

i say i'm not sure i want

to perpetuate

my family's legacy

of gratuitous

self-aggrandizement i mean

i don't say, but mean

all middle-class families

deserve to have art

made about them, right? why else

would they suffer so

their charmed lives wasted on them

as mine is on me

i'm thirty-fucking-three, so

trigger warning: death

you think swimming in the sea's

fun cuz it reminds

us of not yet being born?

trigger warning: death

a high school kid's poem reads

trigger warning: death

is trauma not something you

have to have lived thru?

i guess in life's midst we're in

trigger warning: death

it's coming for you faster

than the island can

receding as it always

seems to be doing

a mausoleum for grief

cumstained rage over

half-remembered gestures in

glittering sunspeak

But who hasn't felt life was

done at 25

or 17 or the age

that Jesus died at

so dissolve me into screens

green avatars rise

up in the boreal dawn

black sun vertigo

there is an architecture

By the youtube fire

thinking of grandparents i've

known / others' i've not

i remember how weird to

be a thing that thinks

that lives & will die as have

others before me

why this body not that one

if the past is so

present in the present like

hydras of being

Suddenly i remember

death is what brought me

to the island in the first

place a 99-

year-old passing so i could

be reborn in its

waters like a mer-phoenix

– is that what i think ? –

my other friend says of it

« what really stood out

is how happy you were there »

are my joys manias

then exuberant high peaks

amidst the long lows

sure don't self-diagnose but

how could the island

not be another symptom

every instance of

its appearance death-coated

a revelation

utterly useless to me

unless it's to say

i'm misguided in all my

moments of being

& if that's the case well then

what to see & know

& yet abstain ? o hell no

And then what about

the extravagant joy that

i am filled with when

you come vast sea of porcelain

curves undulating

unleashed how reality

comes out of nowhere

suddenly asserts itself

in arching light threads

that trace the length of you &

i am so in awe

of your absolute presence

so screw the haunted

demon city of my heart

when we can swim &

dance cormorant-style, sea-drunk

feed stray cats tuna

while silently whale corpses

fall down through the sea

Sometimes it's hard not to think

i peaked at 16

i recall feeling myself

at my most alive

bound to a single purpose

300 of us

on a train to some protest

high on our own smells

keffiyehs draped over the nose

just so u feel me

burnt amber butter b.o.

red maple glimmers

my black matrix coat billowed

i stared hard ahead

thinking i was so at one

with things finally

my friend turned to me & said

dude are you ok ?

So now i’m flung back into

linen pants & snood

Andalusian winter bitch

nice enough to surf

which i do learn how to do

kinda though i used

to think it impossible

kinda i am told

« you cannot be hard surfing

you must be bendy

to become one with the waves

my bro u feel me ? »

& i do or i want to

feel it feelingly

Old friend flies out cuz he's like

all yolo these days

after one of those real life

things that can happen

when you are in your thirties

& god i want him

to lead a beautiful life

to be just flowing

at one with the sea & sun

gold hair flung cackling

& now here he is like yes !

& i'm just like yes !

& we're both just like hell yes !

o sometimes it's just

too much but good like rays of

light in our grey skin

What we want's summer dirty
bare feet in the grass
peach juice drenched bodies ok
so take me to church
melt me in emerald fire
worship is a bad
metaphor for sex because
it's just not that deep
like my voice isn't its twang
hopelessly lacking
in authority but if
you listen baby
i'll make it shake the sky out
for memories of
my new friend running naked
bearded hysteria
into the seafoam screaming
this is paradise
bro come on ! splashing wildly
which would be fine but

i saw the black glint of space

in the pits he calls

eyes vortexes in the sand

i mean how could you

not love the ones who know that

it’s out from the depths

that we call to you o moon

Song of ass & ire :

your messiah complex looks

good in the compost

come pest, bend me into new

horizons gaslit

as green flash we never saw

what happened in that

goddamn rearview mirror but

honestly who cares

about another phantasm

in the grand scheme of

this vast metempsychotic

psychosis of ours

So don't you worry baby

soon we will get to

the island of hopes and dreams

yes heaven on earth

is coming for you & me

no not today no

not yet but soon yes so soon

we have been prepping

the body prepping the mind

all year we're ready

& it's coming for us yes

the long awaited

time to frolic have respite's

coming no we won't

be too old not yet the time

will be just right yes

the strangers will smile at us

yes love us brushing

warmly past us on the beach

fill our hearts with joy

it will happen the moment

has not passed by yet

no we are not rendered back

to our solitude

with only the creaking sound

of the fan to keep

us from forgetting to breathe

the devouring days

When what we want's prostration

tantric funeral

baby i know what i am

dying all over

endlessly divisible

smudged fly on the sheets

not some cosmic vacuum dream

consciousness crap yes

matter over mind baby

i'd love to be all

moon tiara magic bitch

but this world's all there

is & if delirium's

as close as i'll get

to feeling held in the light

so what ? i will have

done some small twisted glory

to the boys who run

unable to extricate

from underbellies

their iron effervescence

& pity the sun

for being all-unseeing

unmoved by holes like

gold fists in dirt saying here

enter my abyss

arpeggios of seething

i don't know much but

i can feel the sea breeze on

my skin saying time

to try & live again to

take the rainbow road

i just want to gorge on stars

So i go outside

bike to some house of the lord

stained glass casts rainbow

shadows on the cool stone floor

& i gaze up at

Michael wielding a huge sword

stepping on Satan's

shoulders as he writhes & squirms

& find i want him

to step on me too Michael

please yes i need you

to Michael step on my face

& send me to hell

- S.S. 2022/2023

Translator's Note

Chania, Crete – October 1st, 2027

True, prior to translating this book, I had heard the name Oscar d'Artois mentioned once or twice in passing. I had even perhaps read the odd poem here and there on the internet at some point in the last decade, if memory serves. Although it's possible I have him mixed up with some other literary debutant named Oscar who'd been flirting with the burgeoning online literary scene at the time, as it seemed there were infinite numbers constantly sprouting up like so many ephemeral early spring dandelions. It was, however, my impression that, like those flowers, he had blossomed and then vanished as others are wont to do back into the sea of literary anonymity, to go pursue whatever corporate or other life he'd found was his actual calling.

In fact, it is almost certainly due to this that the manuscript initially caught my eye.

While on vacation last October in Chania, on the island of Crete, trying to prolong the rays of the Indian summer for just a tad bit longer (while the struggles of being an independent contractor on the translation market are many – loneliness, chasing after clients, burdensome taxes – there are granted a few perks), I took a digestive stroll after having just enjoyed a delectable halloumi gyro sandwich at Pita Goal, a friendly mom & pop establishment with a wonderful atmosphere (my side order of *tzatziki* came out of the kitchen decorated like a face: two olives, cucumbers for ears, a red pepper slice for lips… Setting it down on the table the doyenne declared: "Your Tzatziki is monkey!"). I ambled my way down to the scenic old Venetian port and was poking my head into this or that trinket shop, when I came across a bookstore called, simply, Mediterraneo Bookstore. It was clearly aimed at tourists, selling mainly postcards and books about Cretan and ancient Minoan history, but, hoping perhaps to find a few English translations of some young Greek contemporary authors, I decided to pop in.

It was here that I stumbled upon a manuscript, handwritten and in the original French, to my astonishment, placed squarely between copies of Cavafy's *Selected Poems* and Borges's *Garden of Forking Paths,* both in English translations. The cover read simply: *L'Île – Oscar d'Artois.* As far as I could tell, there was only one copy there, and it was the only book in French in the entire store. It was either handwritten or typed up in such a way as to seem handwritten (I confess I had accepted the small shot of Raki I had been offered complimentarily by the Pita mistress at the end of my meal, so my perception may not have been the clearest). There were holes in several pages in the back of the manuscript, so it was by no means a brand-new copy. If anything, it was as if it had been placed there as a ruse by some roguish type – and, indeed, when I looked at the back there was no price tag, and when I went up to the register to pay for it the clerk simply looked at me in bemusement. So I bought a few Minotaur postcards and made hastily away with the book before they started asking too many questions.

To my knowledge, any work of d'Artois's I had previously encountered had been in English. I had not been aware of any translation efforts. Curious, then, I found the town beach, plopped down, and promptly began my perusal. While I found the poem odd at times, it did pique a certain interest in me – enough so anyway that, in a flurry of excitement, I sprang up, ran back to my room for pen and paper (well, electronic tablet), pulled up to my writing desk and, in a sort of fever-pitch, spent the night jotting down a quick translation of the entire book.

While prey to this frenzy, I also found the form the poem takes – verses alternating in a 5/7/5/7/5/7/5 syllabic pattern – to be rather addictive, and noticed I was beginning to think in the form, so much so that I even began playing around with drafting a few quick lines of my own, such as:

« Your tzatziki is monkey! »
the pita pocket
lady says : olives for eyes
cucumber slice ears
i want to tip her the world

or:

licking the dregs of
an empty aioli pot
like a feral cat

or:

desperately trying
to get a double rainbow
pic – storage full though
also it is pouring rain

Unfortunately, back at my hotel the following day, as I was lying on a beach bed, sun-kissed or perhaps slightly sun-burnt and trying to escape the rays under a parasol, having just finished scribbling down the final notes for an English version on my tablet, and rather carelessly I must admit, I lay the original manuscript down in the sand and promptly fell into a well-warranted *siesta.*

What I had failed to notice was that no more than a dozen feet away was a large anthill and - perhaps due to the small amount of sweet Retsina wine I may have inadvertently spilled on it - by the time I awoke the sun was going down and the manuscript was completely covered in ants. In my panic, I did my best to shoo them away with my beach hat and the assistance of the friendly barman's broom, but by the time I had managed to make most of them clear off, it was obvious they had done irrevocable damage to the manuscript – that is to say, it had been devoured almost in its entirety by the ants, leaving behind only a few fragmentary scraps of paper, which naturally I hastened to assemble.

I must, however, confess that I fear certain parts of the work may have been forever lost. For the notes for a translation I had jotted down were just that, notes, and I most likely overlooked certain parts – though I have marked out as best I could, via page breaks, the parts where there may be lacunae, as the text that I myself read was wholly uninterrupted, simply one long string of unrelenting text.

This led to several problems, not the least of which is that the occasional fragment would turn up whose placement within the poem I was not quite sure of, such as:

i'm not saying i want to
die but if i did
i guess i wouldn't mind if
it were down here on
the river's floodplain where in
between the post-rain
green soil smell & roiling place
sky & river meet
i can feel infinity

And – to be perfectly honest – I am not entirely sure whether he himself wrote those lines or if I did, caught up as I was in the sort of emulative daze I previously mentioned.

In an attempt to resolve these issues, I took to the internet's search engines, and looked up and tried to contact d'Artois himself, to recover the missing manuscript pieces, clarify their order, and ask a few questions about the meaning behind specific terms. But I was roundly ignored. I have therefore done my best with what I had on hand, in a way I hope is most reflective of the original.

All the other information that I could find about him consisted in a few old poems – no more than you can count on your fingers – published in online literary reviews, many of them now defunct and the links to them broken, and what seemed to be a few chaotic rants and questions on online yoga forums relating to Vedic concepts and the best way to access this or that pose. My various unanswered emails coupled with his seeming lack of an online presence these days led me to question whether d'Artois was even still with us at all.

The problems that arise when attempting to transmute this text into the English language are varied and manifold:

- First and foremost is of course the matter of the form, a sort of broken, ongoing haiku – how is one to translate both form and content? I have done my best.
- Then, there is the not-small problem of the sole extant copy having been devoured by ants. Any perceived fragmentary or chaotic nature to the text should thus perhaps be imputed to Nature herself rather than to an issue of the internal organization within the original poem.
- Then, there is cultural content that simply doesn't translate: are people aware, for instance, outside of France, that it is possible to ask for a half baguette in any bakery there? Or that the chrysanthemum is a flower that has a strong association with death, and is traditionally reserved for funerals or laying on graves?
- And then, there is the queasiness one cannot help but feel upon reading sudden outbursts of homoerotic yearning coming from a fellow who, by his own admission, is clearly married – still, uncouth as it may seem, one must translate it.
- And there is another discomfort, too, for a die-hard agnostic such as me – that is, the seeming recurring

obsession with God, in a way that makes it difficult not to wonder whether d'Artois's isn't yet another brain more damaged by organized religion than perhaps even he is aware. But again, one cannot simply up and say this, as it is the role of the translator to vanish behind the varnish of the text.

- There is also a tendency within d'Artois's writing to veer into a "text message" or "online chat" style of vernacular shorthand common to today's youth (to which, frankly, he himself barely belongs). Whether he does this out of some pretense at poetic hyper-concision, out of affectation to make himself seem more "of the people," or simply out of laziness, remains unclear. Annoying though it may seem to some, I have nevertheless endeavored to preserve this stylistic quirk, allowing for creative misspellings now and again (I have not bothered to attempt internal consistency, as d'Artois himself seemingly does not).
- It should also be noted that, in the French, d'Artois occasionally "smudges" his own syllable count, if for instance there is some ambiguity as to whether a word containing two vowels in a row is monosyllabic or duo-syllabic, as well as at other times where pronunciation might differ from the technical written count or between individuals. As a result, I have granted myself the same liberty, making the daunting task of matching the syllabic count of a poem of this length in another language slightly less so. I must beg for the punctilious reader's indulgence in this matter. Examples of vowel-shortening include words like "poem" or "mania." Likewise, I have occasionally made words longer than the way one might pronounce them if the written count allows for this, as in "clinically" or "giggling." There are also words like "power," "tower," or "listening," which should sometimes be

read as if they contained the apostrophe used e.g. in early modern English writing to shorten verse: pow'r, tow'r, list'ning, etc. I have omitted the apostrophes themselves for fear of rendering the text illegible to the modern lay reader.

- Penultimately, there is the matter of the point d'Artois is trying to get at. He seems to build his way up from an absolute miasma of chaos & confusion into a sort of messy, inverted cosmogony over the course of the hundred-odd pages the poem runs on for – affirming something like a primacy of the material over the spiritual. But why, one cannot help but wonder, does it take him so long? It takes Valéry about 150 lines to make a similar point in *The Graveyard by the Sea*. Why does it take d'Artois some 1,500? Is there something else going on here? Are there subtleties I have missed? He never answered my emails, and so perhaps we'll never know.
- Finally, beyond the mere problem of translating it from the language of one place to that of another, there was what I experienced as a problem of periodicity. Indeed, at the time of d'Artois's writing – he dates it to the early 2020s – there was an idea floating around that writing mattered only for the living, for those who could read a text when it came out, a demand for an immediacy in literature. This is something he seems to have been aware of, and yet there is clearly also an obsession in his poem with timelessness, with wanting to create something whose relevance might just go beyond the next few weeks or season, the sort of writing one could describe as being concerned with "the universal human condition" – which, as I mentioned, was rather out of favor at the time. To attempt to transpose this sentiment, even now, feels – to use modern parlance – rather cringe, especially without being able to know just how sincere his efforts in

this direction were meant. Still, it felt unfair to the poem to completely ignore this aspect, so I have endeavored to render both its "contemporary" flavor and its hungry eye for eternity.

While I found myself unable to reach the poet himself, I did manage, via word of mouth and by inquiring across my various networks, to find another who had translated d'Artois's works before (among the many nasty twists of his character, one is that d'Artois is a writer who seems to almost invariably not give credit where credit is due to those who humbly reproduce his œuvre into other languages, a practice that is most frowned upon within the industry!). This person spoke to me on the condition of anonymity, as they did not wish to associate their name with that of the elusive poet (and so perhaps it was that they requested not to be credited, after all). In confidence, then, they told me via email that when having an exchange with him, once, and struggling to untangle what one might call the various metaphysical arguments – regarding the body, death, the soul's existence and separateness or lack thereof, etc. – battling it out within another longer piece of his, that finally, in exasperation or impatience, d'Artois had simply replied: "It's only a goddamn poem."

- Christopher Seder

This text is indebted to and/or rips off:

Caroline Rayner, SOPHIE, Ted Rees, John Milton, Caroline Polachek, Alice Notley, Rainer Maria Rilke, Freckle, Abd al Malik, Henning Lundkvist, Sam Riviere, Hannah Diamond, Frank O'Hara, David Berman, Mike Young/Madonna, Oneohtrix Point Never, Anne Carson, Bladee, Adam Mann of News from Science Magazine, Yung Lean, Gabby Bess aka Goddess Earth, Paul Valéry, Philip Pullman, Klara Puski, Cascada, Robert Jordan, Author of deaf-gay-techno-punk YA novel whose name I can't remember or find anywhere online, Kristen Felicetti, CROOK, Miss Kittin, Niki Schur-Narula, Sheila Byers, Agnès Varda, Steven Patrick Morrissey, Samuel Light, Brian Boisvert, Mylène Farmer, Chloé Caldwell, Terrence Malick, Louise Trueheart, Perfume Genius, boygenius, Mary Oliver, River Phoenix & Keanu Reeves, Dennis Cooper, Zac Farley, Tristan Tzara, Danny L. Harle, Danuta Borchardt, Austin Mitchell aka 'It's a whole vibe' guy, Rachelle Toarmino, Aidan Ryan, Antonin Artaud, Kimberly Jannarone, Curro Arroyo, Arthur Rimbaud, Manuel Bedoya, Mitski, Emily Dickinson, Hafiz, Francisque-Joseph Duret, Virginia Woolf, Arca, Alvaro Alvarez, Zeno, Liz Bowen, Will Glovinsky, Unreliable Eurotrash, Ulíses de Miguel-Rodriguez, William Shakespeare, Mad Manning, Lucy K Shaw, & others I have missed.

An initial version of it was set to piano & performed at Peter BD's gallery show 'ETC.' in Manhattan in June 2023.

Thank you to all of you <3

Oscar d'Artois is a writer & translator who was born in 1989 in Paris, France. He is also the author of *Teen Surf Goth* (Metatron, 2015) and lives mostly out of a suitcase.

Mad Manning is a Berlin based visual artist and tattooer who uses surrealist imagery to explore emotional experience and human connection.

They met in first grade.

@oscardartois @madmanware

For the secret liner notes to this book, visit:
shabbydollhouse.com/tower

ALSO FROM

SHABBY DOLL HOUSE

LOG OFF

by Kristen Felicetti

SALMON

by Sebastian Castillo

THE MOAN WILDS

by Caroline Rayner

WOMAN WITH HAT

by Lucy K Shaw

WE DIE IN ITALY

by Sarah Jean Alexander

TROISIEME VAGUE

by Lucy K Shaw

COMING SOON

???

www.ingramcontent.com/pod-product-compliance
Lightning Source LLC
Chambersburg PA
CBHW060608080526
44585CB00013B/734
9781737924265